Úrsula Calderón
Cristina Calderón

HAI KUR MAMÁŠU ČIS

I want to tell you a story

Written by
Cristina Zárraga

Woodcuts by
Jimena Saiter

Translated to English by
Jacqueline Windh

HAI KUR MAMÁŠU ČIS
I want to tell you a story

English language edition

© 2013 Ediciones Pix
Ukika, Chile

Woodcuts
© 2005 Jimena Saiter

Translation to English
© 2013 Jacqueline Windh

Graphic design
© 2013 Oliver Vogel

All rights reserved
No part of this book may be used or reproduced in any manner whatsoever without written permission except in the case of brief quotations embodied in critical articles and reviews. For information: ediciones-pix@yagan.org

Printed by CreateSpace in 2013

ISBN 978-1492180593

Authorized translation from the
original Spanish language edition
HAI KUR MAMÁŠU ČIS
Quiero contarte un cuento
© 2005 Cristina Zárraga
RPI 134.789
© 2007 Ediciones Pix, Ukika, Chile
ISBN 978-956-310-939-9

In memory of Úrsula Calderón

TABLE OF CONTENTS

Preface — *12*

Introduction to the English Edition — *16*

The Yagan people — *18*

I

Tuín or Black-Chinned Siskin	23
Kuštéata or Sea-Lion	27
Pána or Cormorant	31
Káyuš or Guanaco	37
Lána or Giant Woodpecker	41

II

Laxúwa or Ibis	47
Hašpúl or Diucon bird	51
Šakóa or Snipe	53

III

Hánnuš	57
Hánnuš and the Boy	61
Hánnuš and the Woman	65

IV

Táun or Glaciers	71
Akasiř or Thrush	75
Tačikáčina or Rayadito	79
Hainóla or Orca	81
Luš yámana or Shining Man	83

PREFACE

A spiritual and illusory world... of beings living firmly grounded in the natural world yet before the presence of *Watauinéiwa*, calling upon the elements, and the animals and the birds – and the birds, raising their wings, granted responses as omens.

Hai kur mamášu čis or "I want to tell you a story," as the Yagan grandmothers used to refer to their story-telling, is a journey through the landscape of the Yagan of old: a unique culture, rich in character, customs and beliefs. These stories take place below this same sky and over these same waters, in giant voyaging canoes and around eternal fires and on immense mountains. A landscape which has always been open to the passage of humankind...

Mamášu čis is the time when birds used to be humans, perhaps also the time before there was an understanding of all that exists, of even ourselves. The stories from these times – myths, legends and beliefs – bring us closer to the core of human nature, to our deepest levels of being. The deeds, the values and anti-values, the tricks and heroic actions, all lead to the transformations, to the idea of some sort of beginning.
These stories take us back to the times of the ancestors, when winged beings and the other animals existed in their essence.

Tášix said, "I am going to be penguin." But he who, in reality, would become the penguin, answered, "You cannot, you are too small. You are *tášix*."

Tášix, the little bird that in English is called cinclodes, is also known as the pilot bird, because his shape reminds us of *šúša* the penguin.

This knowledge has been collected through conversations and story-telling with two Yagan women, my grandmother Cristina Calderón and her sister, now gone, Úrsula Calderón.

They say that the following transformation happened in a place called *Íaiošáka*.

There was a lake near there, in which two girls were bathing and talking, speaking of forbidden things, when suddenly they were surprised by *lăm*, the sun. Ashamed, the two girls hid their heads under the water, and they turned into *malápa*, or lake ducks. Since then, they have lived in the lakes, hiding their heads under the water whenever they are surprised.

Íaiošáka today is the location of Ushuaia's airport, on the island of Tierra del Fuego.

The first five stories are transformation stories, where humans turn into birds – as happens with the siskins, the women who find themselves liberated from the giant and turn into *tuín*. Transformations take place in other stories, too, resulting from tragic events and displays of animal nature, such as the story of *pána*, or cormorant.

The stories in Part II tell us how children should behave around the birds, based upon Cristina's own experiences: if we see the *hašpúl*, we should not throw stones at him, because he is a bird of bad omen.

Part III tells stories of *hannuś*, the monkey-man who was feared by Yagan, and who spoke their same language. *Hánnuś* used to live on Hoste Island, where today we can see *Hánnuś Arkuř*, or Monkey Rock, the rock which *hánnuś* became when he was surprised by a *yámana*.

The final stories relate to specific beliefs of the Yagan people. Inside the icebergs lived spirits, which is why icebergs were feared and respected when people were paddling near them. "I believe it, because I have seen it," said my Aunt Úrsula.

Hai kur mamášu čis is ancient wisdom, stories passed down orally since the beginning of time by the ancestors, and passed down today through the voices of my grandmothers.

Watauinéiwa | The ancient one, God.

Ikamánakípa | Woman who writes

ACKNOWLEDGEMENTS

To my great-aunt Úrsula Calderón who, through her memories, allowed us to record stories that were told to her, as well as stories that she herself lived. And to whom this work is dedicated.

To my grandmother Cristina Calderón, who introduced me to these stories through her memories, her experiences, and her language. Stories that share with us the wisdom of the Yagan people.

To all of my Yagan family, for allowing me to listen to, explore, and compile the voices of our ancestral culture, and for giving me the opportunity to live with them and with my grandmothers in Ukika, Navarino Island, since 2001.

To Jimena Saiter, for her work on the xylographs, over long days and short days on Navarino, creating illustrations in wood that interpret each story.

To my friend Jacqueline Windh, who gave birth to the idea of translating Hai kur mamášu čis to English. I thank her for her work as a translator, for her perserverance in bringing this edition to publication, and above all for her patience as we worked together to create this new revised edition.

To my beloved Oliver Vogel, who also was part of this Spanish-English revision, for his time and his suggestions, and also for his work designing this book.

Thanks to the many who collaborated indirectly in the production of this book.

Cristina Zárraga
Ikamánakípa

INTRODUCTION TO THE ENGLISH EDITION

I have always been intrigued by ocean-going canoes. I like to believe that this perhaps is due to some sort of genetic memory, a result of my pure Viking ancestry.

When I discovered that canoeing peoples inhabited the canals and fiords of southern Patagonia, and that these cultures bore many similarities to the canoeing people where I live, on Vancouver Island in North America's Pacific northwest, I resolved to meet them.

My travels took me to Navarino Island, to the southernmost human settlements on our planet aside from Antarctic research bases: the small and isolated naval town of Puerto Williams, and the tiny Yagan village alongside it, Ukika. I soon met Cristina Zárraga who, at the time, was in the midst of working with her grandmother on the first Spanish edition of HAI KUR MAMÁŠU ČIS.

Cristina shared the stories in her work-in-progress with me. I was struck by the parallels between the traditional stories of the Yagan people and those of North America's west coast cultures: origin stories that explain features of the landscape; transformation stories from times long ago when the animals and birds had human forms; even stories featuring a sort of Sasquatch or Bigfoot, a giant monkey-man known in the Yagan language as *hánnuš*.

I was convinced that these stories should be shared with a larger audience, and I offered to translate them to English. I am grateful to Cristina for accepting my offer; for the trust that she gave to me by allowing me to become a part of this project; for the kindness and generosity of her family members on Navarino; and especially for the friendship that she and I now share.

Jacqueline Windh
Port Alberni, Vancouver Island, 2013

THE YAGAN PEOPLE

The Yagan or *Yámana* of Patagonia, the southernmost indigenous group in the world, were a canoe-going people. Their traditional territory is the cold and turbulent waters south of Tierra del Fuego, and the islands southward all the way to Cape Horn.

The Patagonian landscape is reminiscent of North America's Pacific northwest. Yagan territory is the same latitude south of the equator as Sitka, Alaska, is to the north. Narrow canals and inlets cut the steep forested shores into a jigsaw puzzle of peninsulas and islands. Snow-capped mountains hang overhead, spawning glaciers which descend to the sea and feed icebergs into the fiords.

It was through these waters that, for thousands of years, the Yagan – fishers, hunters, nomadic families – paddled tiny canoes stitched together from strips of bark of the coigüe tree. They slept in huts covered with sea-lion skins or branches, which they could construct quickly upon stopping at a beach for the night. They carried their fire in their canoes with them, smouldering upon a bed of mud and sand. The women typically paddled the canoes, and swam naked in the frigid waters to anchor the canoes in kelp beds, and gathered foods such as berries and shellfish. The men were typically the hunters, going after sea-lions or fish from the canoes, or hunting in the hills for guanaco, a type of wild llama.

The Yagan language is rich in its range and complexity. Cristina Calderón is its only remaining native speaker, and she is also the last pure-blooded member of the Yagan people.

Today, an international border passes through the core of traditional Yagan territory, down the centre of the Beagle Channel. A few dozen descendents of the Yagan people live on the Chilean side of that border, on Navarino Island, in a small village called Ukika.

I

TUÍN OR BLACK-CHINNED SISKIN

When we were little girls, they used to tell us not to become too attached to any stick or rock or any other thing like that – or it might turn into a person.

And that is what happened to one little girl. She took a pretty stone, which she had found at *Tašuáni*, on the seashore, and she kept saying to it, "This is my baby." She cared for it like a baby, until one day it turned itself into a real baby boy. It grew a little head, and hands and feet, but his body remained of stone. She always carried him with her, and she gave him her breast – until one day he bit her, and pulled her nipple right off.

So the father of the little girl said, "This thing is evil, we can't keep it with us. What we're going to do is throw him into the water," and they flung him into the sea.

Sure that he was dead, they went back to their camp. But that afternoon, the little stone baby came back too, wanting to be with his mother.

This little boy grew up. He became a huge man, a giant. He would catch the women who were crossing the channel in their canoes and keep them, and he chased away or killed any man who tried to oppose him.

He had many women. This was over there, in *Lum*. And up on the mountain *Umašapuliak*, this giant used to pull up huge trees by the roots, and he would carry them down over his shoulder so his women could eat the digüeñes, the tree mushrooms growing on them.

One day, up on the mountain, a thorn got stuck in his foot, and he became sick. "Ay, how my foot hurts!" he cried. "Get this thorn out of me!"

He lay down on the pampa, and the women used an *ámi*, a needle made of bone, to dig around in the area where the thorn was. They dug so it hurt, and the giant cried out and complained.

It was a beautiful sunny day, and he fell asleep there. And the women decided to burn him up. They piled the very trees that he had carried down from the mountain around him.

The branches were dry and the fire blazed.

His head and hands and feet all burnt. But his body, which was made of stone, started to split apart. Small stones jumped out of the fire, and the women used sticks to poke them back in.

And the women, when they touched those stones, they turned into *tuín*, the little siskin birds, those ones that fly together in a flock crying out their song, happy to be liberated from that giant.

You used to be able to see, over there in *Lum*, a rock that reminded us of that giant. Also, it is said that if you light a fire near that place, the little stones all start to burst open.

Umašapuliak | A mountain known for all the calafate bushes with big thorns, the kind of thorn that hurt the stone giant.

Ámi | A bird bone sharpened to a point, used to weave baskets from reeds.

KUŠTÉATA OR SEA-LION

Two sisters were on the seashore, watching the waves. The younger sister announced that she had seen a sea-lion. The older one had actually been exchanging glances with this sea-lion, but she pretended that she did not believe her sister.

The three of them continued at this game for several days, and soon the older sister and the sea-lion had fallen in love. One day the sea-lion came, hidden inside a wave, and he took the girl away with him.

When the younger sister figured out what had happened, she returned to the camp to tell her family.

Time passed. The sea-lion and the girl married. They formed a family, conceiving a son who had a head like his mother's, but the body of a sea-lion.

One day, *kuštéata* the sea-lion asked his wife if he could meet her family. She had always worried about such a meeting, because she didn't think that her family would approve of her choice of mate. However, she could not go against the wishes of her husband, the sea-lion.

Soon, the couple found themselves camped alongside the girl's family.

And after a few days, one morning, the mother invited the girl to go gather shellfish with her. However, the girl did not trust her brothers and sisters, and she was afraid to leave her husband with them. But her mother insisted, saying that her brothers and sisters all loved the sea-lion.

So they took off in the canoe. And when they were far away, the girl started to hear the cries of the sea-lion. She wanted to go back, but her mother calmed her, saying, "Don't worry, they're only playing."

Arriving back at camp, they found her young son with a slice of meat in his hands. He was singing, "How delicious, my father's flesh that I am eating." He had fallen under the influence of his aunts and uncles who, with his mother gone, had killed the sea-lion and cooked him up.

His mother, in great despair, took a sea-urchin and threw it at her son's forehead, turning him into *káyes*, that fish that carries on its forehead the mark of the urchin thrown by his mother.

Káyes | Also called the kelp fish, because it is found in the kelp beds.

PÁNA OR CORMORANT

Grandmother Emilia told me this story...

Once upon a time there was a couple and their daughter. The daughter was already grown up, and she was still single. Unfortunately for her, *pána* fell in love with her.

Every time her parents left to go fishing, this man came by to pester the girl, asking, "Are you going to marry me or not?" and the girl would cry. She would cover herself up with branches, with grass – she didn't want to marry him.

So there came a day when her parents, as usual, left the camp to gather food. *Pána* watched them go, and decided to take advantage of their absence. He went to *Tašuáni* to look for a stone.

He was thinking, "I will kill that girl. She doesn't want to be with me, I'm going to kill her."

He went back to the girl and he asked her again, "Are you coming with me now or not?" She hid her face and cried. All the while, *pána* was heating up the stone in the fire and repeating, "Are you coming with me? I want to marry you."

He heated the stone until it was red-hot, then he violently grabbed the girl. He put the stone into her, burning her completely inside. And by doing that, he killed her. Then, raising his wings, he left that place.

The cormorant flew up to a cliff and waited. He watched as the parents made their way back to their home.

And looking at them, he started to call, "Go see your daughter now. Yes, you go and take good care of her."

The parents asked one another, "Why would that bird say that?"

Arriving home, they found their daughter dead and they figured out what had happened. The father, distraught, said to his wife, "We are going to find someone with a sling-shot, someone who will kill that cormorant."

And so they did. They asked around, trying to find a brave person who could kill that horrible bird. But it wasn't easy. No one was able to kill that cormorant, because he was always up so high.

They went to Remolino, looking for someone to help. A small man stepped forward and volunteered to confront that bird. The little man armed his sling-shot. The first stone didn't reach high enough, and the cormorant laughed and made fun of him. The next stone went too high, and the bird laughed even more. And the third stone hit the cormorant right in the middle of the head, and down he fell.

Everyone who was watching ran around on the ground looking for the cormorant. They found him in his final death throes. They cut his body up into little pieces, and started tossing them around.

And those pieces, as they fell down, they turned into little cormorants. Those little birds flocked together and flew away from that place.

It is said that the families who were around, watching what had happened from their canoes, all started paddling quickly, making lots of big waves, and from that time onward we have known *Ašáka* or Molinares as a bay with rough turbulent waters.

And also, since then we have known *pána* the cormorant in his normal size, much smaller than the bird of this story. And the parents of the girl, they turned into *kalála* or seagulls.

KÁYUŠ OR GUANACO

Once upon a time there was a family: the father, the mother, and their two daughters.

The girls grew up and one day the mother died, leaving the two girls in the care of their father. After some time, the father developed the desire to join himself as a man with his daughters. Once the girls figured out his intentions, they took to running away every time he came near.

This situation drove the father to pretend that he was very sick, with a sickness that soon would take him to his death. He asked the girls, when they buried him after he died, to cover only his body but not his face.

And so the father managed to deceive his daughters. After his supposed death, they were both very sad. They took charcoal and ground it up and painted their faces. They both cried as they buried him in the way that he had requested, thus complying with their father's wish.

While the girls were crying, the father got up and stood in front of them.

Frightened and surprised, they cried, "My father!" But he answered, "I am not your father, your father died. I am here to marry you both."

He threw himself on top of them, and when they got up they all turned into *amára* or guanacos, and they ran together and disappeared into the mountains, where we can still see them today.

Amára | Guanacos (wild llamas) in general.

Káyuš | A male guanaco.

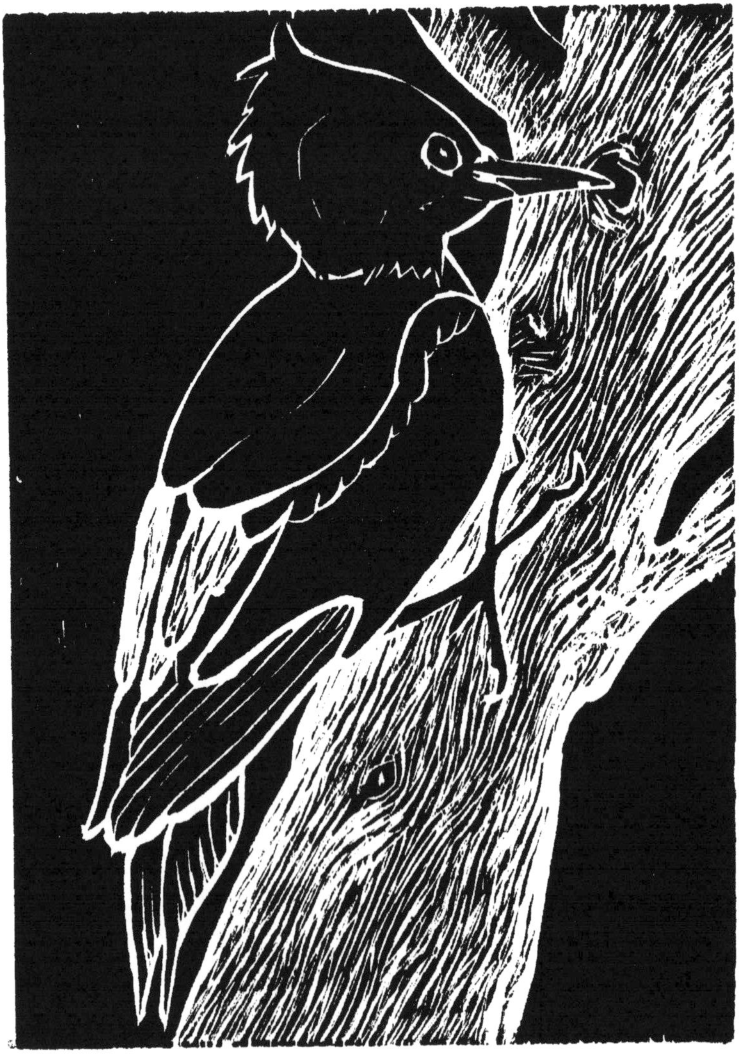

LÁNA OR GIANT WOODPECKER

It is said that, in the times when birds were humans, a young boy fell in love with his sister. He was always trying to find excuses to entice her out of her *ákař*, so he could be with her. But his sister was wise to his intentions. She hid from her brother each time that he went looking for her, so she could avoid relations which are prohibited.

One day in the forest, the boy found some huge red *amáim* or chaura berries, and he went looking for his sister to tell her. She took her basket and went into the forest searching for the berries. Meanwhile, her brother went ahead to a place that he knew she would have to pass by, and he hid there.

When she came close, he threw himself at her and embraced her. Together, they fell to the ground, releasing themselves to their love. And when they got up, they turned into birds and flew away like *lána*, the giant woodpeckers.

Ever since then, they have lived together in the forests, and the brother has a red crest on the top of his head recalling the colour of those big red *amáim* berries.

Ákař | Hut

II

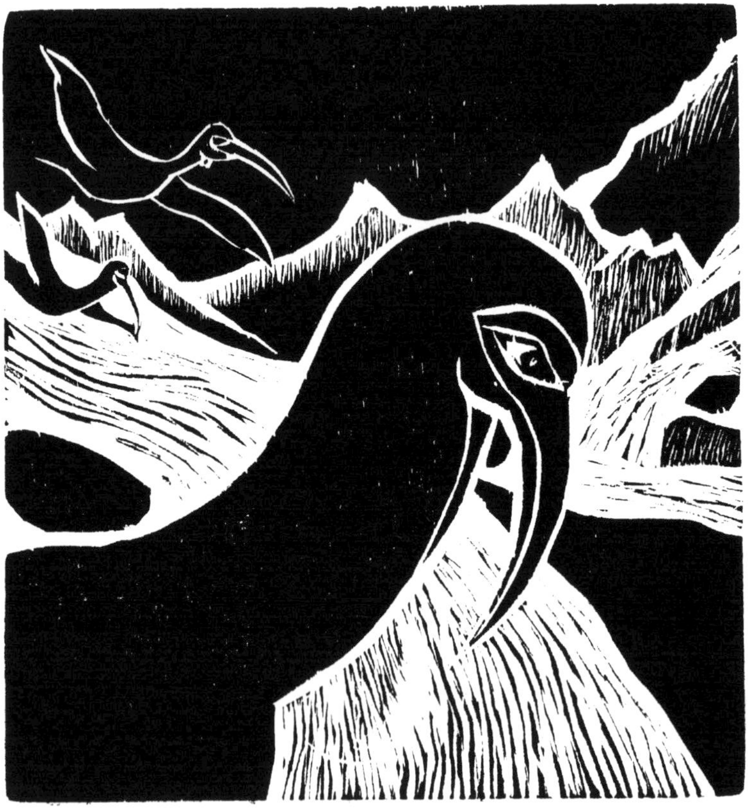

LAXÚWA OR IBIS

One day, as spring was arriving, a *yámana* stuck his head out of his *ákař* and saw a *laxúwa* flying in the sky. The *yámana* was so happy that he shouted to the others, "An ibis is flying over our *ákař*, look!" Immediately the others came out of their *ákařs* crying, "Spring has arrived, the ibis are coming back!" They jumped up and down with joy.

Hearing these cries, the ibis became furious. She was deeply offended, so she conjured up a wild blizzard.

It snowed without cease. It was very cold. All of the land and all of the waters became covered with ice – everything froze.

Many people died, because they were not able to use their canoes to look for food. They could not go out of their *ákařs* to get firewood either, because everything was covered with snow. And so, many people died.

After a very long time, it stopped snowing and the sun started to shine, bringing with it a warmth that melted the ice and snow that had covered all of the land. And so, huge amounts of water started to flow.

The ice melted from the narrow canals and the wide channels, and the Yagan could once again paddle their canoes and go collecting food.

However, on the great mountain slopes and high valleys, the ice was so thick that the warmth of the sun could not melt it.

Even today you can still see the big ice sheets, that descend to the sea and remind us of that severe freeze and blizzard that the *laxúwa* started.

Ever since then, the Yagan treat the ibis with much respect. They say that the ibis is a sensitive and delicate woman, and she likes to be treated with courtesy and deference.

And when ibis come close to camp, the people remain still and silent, especially the children, who are not allowed to imitate their call.

Yámana | Man, alive

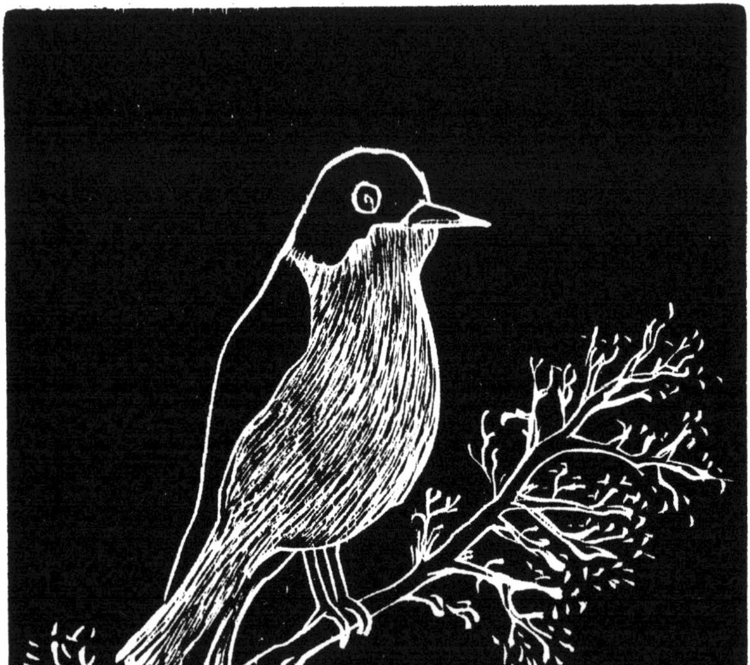

HAŠPÚL OR DIUCON BIRD

My grandfather used to say that *hašpúl*, the little diucon bird, was a bird of bad omen. If we saw one, we were not to throw stones at him. For if we did, *hašpúl* would bring rain, thunder and snow.

My brothers didn't believe our grandfather, so they threw stones at *hašpúl* to see if it was true, what he said. And soon the bad weather started – it brought rain and thunder. "Ohh," they said, "it's true what our grandfather said, we will never do that again."

Later, my mother told us, "When your grandfather says something, we must obey him, because he knows. And besides, it is bad to throw stones at the *hašpúl* bird."

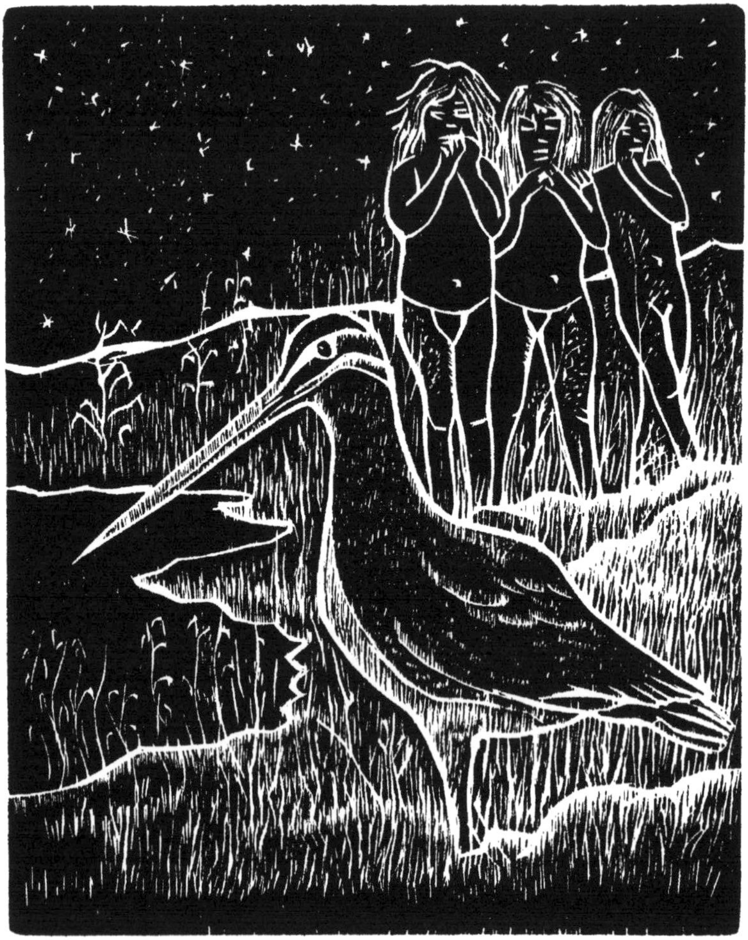

ŠAKÓA OR SNIPE

My parents and my grandparents used to tell us that we should not mimic the *šakóa*, or snipe, when it was flying at night. "If you imitate this bird," they would say, "he will cut your toe with grass fibres, or *kuruk*."

Since we were stubborn girls, and because when you are a child you always want to try things to see if they are true or not, we wrapped our feet with thick rags and then put socks over top of them. And then we three girls decided to imitate the *šakóa* that night.

The next day we woke up with our feet in great pain, and we realized that we must obey what our parents say, because it was all true.

III

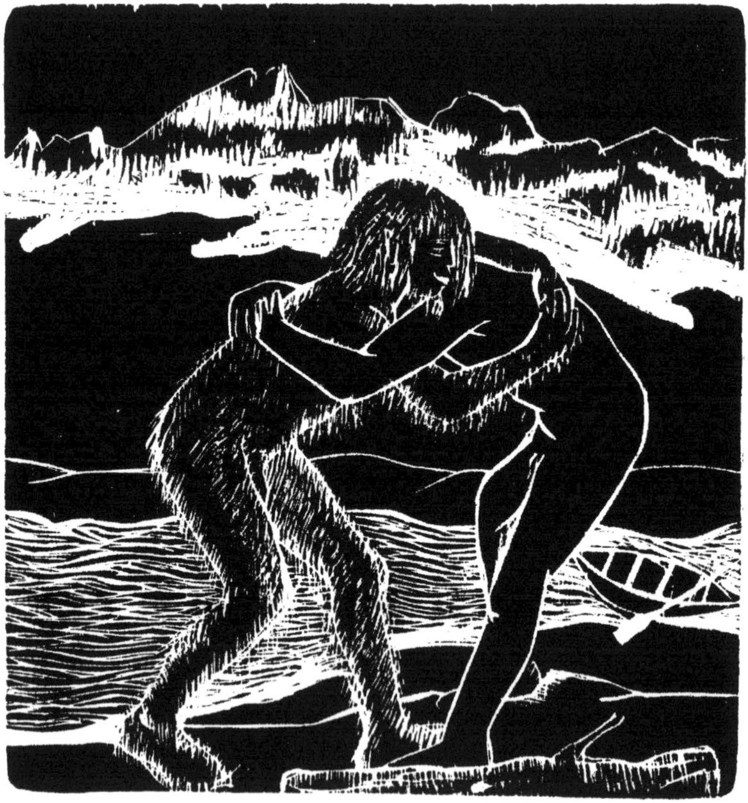

HÁNNUŠ

When voyaging, many Yagan were afraid to land their canoes at the seashore, because they knew of the existence of *hánnuš*.

Hánnuš were like a type of monkey, big and strong, and they always lived alone up in the mountains, hiding, and always watching for the arrival of the Yagan.

One day, *Alapáinš* and his wife *Kărpa Koli Kípa* crossed the channel and went up the mountain in search of digüeñes, the tree mushroooms. *Alapáinš* tied the canoe by the edge of the beach and went up into the forest, while his wife stayed and took care of the fire.

The fire went out, and just at that moment *Kărpa Koli Kípa* had a bad feeling because she heard the song of *tačikáčina*, the little bird who announces the presence of *hánnuš*.

Alapáinš was up in a tree, collecting digüeñes, when suddenly a harsh voice came up to his ears, saying – *iár hípi mamuláko kána ru sa nóna*, "Now we are going to fight, and we will see who wins."

Upon hearing this challenge, *Alapáinš* launched himself back down to the ground so he could run away, because he could well imagine who it was there, challenging him. But *hánnuš* didn't let him get away. He caught him and they started to fight, until *Alapáinš* became tired and came up with the idea of playing dead. So that's what he did.

When *hánnuš* saw that his opponent had stopped moving, he dropped him. And seeing him stretched out on the ground, *hánnuš* started to cry, sad for what he had done. And then he said – *anusafanar*, "You died!" – *hai yenkute sa pafafana*, "I didn't think that you were going to die."

Very sad, *hánnuš* pulled up all the branches he could find, and he used them to cover the body of *Alapáinš*. Then, still crying, he left.

Alapáinš, once he could tell that *hánnuš* was gone, lept up and ran down to where his wife was waiting.

Arriving there, terrified, he jumped into the canoe. *Kărpa Koli Kípa* either knew or guessed what had happened, and she was waiting for him. She started to paddle as fast as possible and they left that place.

Alapáinš | Grandfather of Cristina and Ursula Calderón

Tačikáčina | small songbird, the rayadito (see page 79)

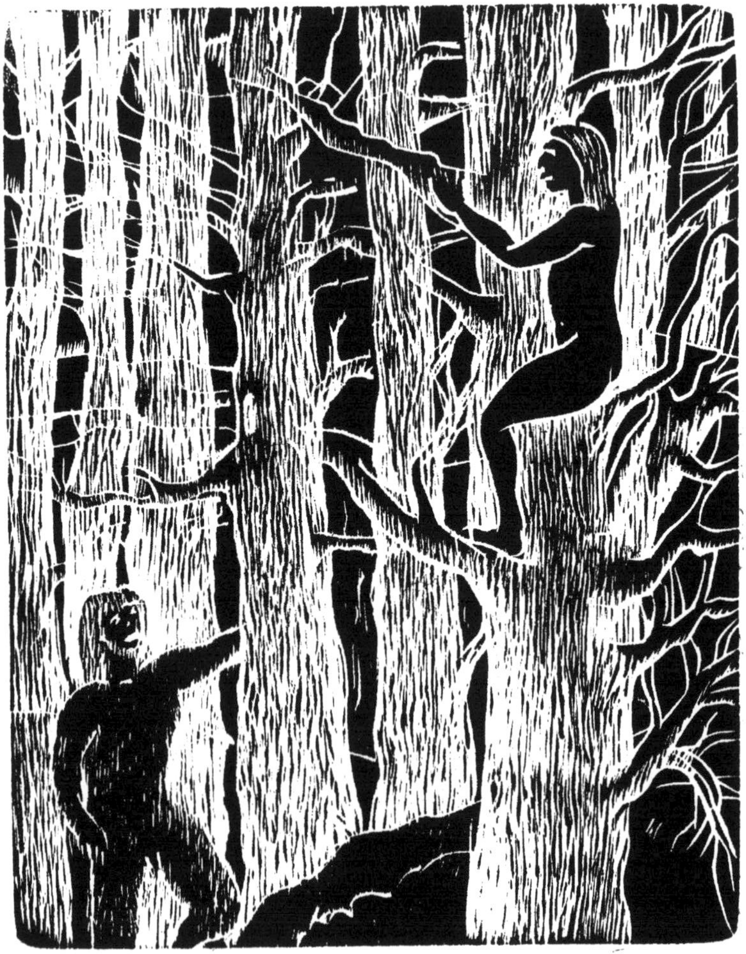

HÁNNUŠ AND THE BOY

The *hánnuš* lived on Hoste Island, and they spoke the same language as the Yagan.

They were very feared, especially by the women and the children, who they would kidnap and keep with them.

One very dark and cold night, a night with a chill that pierced the nostrils, a couple and their small son were travelling in their canoe. Looking for a place where they could stop on such a hellish night, they landed at the edge of a beach. The father got out first, and quickly started to make a hut out of branches, while the mother, holding the child, kept themselves warm by the fire inside the canoe. After a time, strong arms reached in for the child and she handed him over. Then she unloaded their things and brought the fire from the canoe over to the hut.

When she got there, she saw that the boy was not there. So she asked her husband where he was, since he had come to get him some time ago.

They both looked at one another, terrified with the realization that they were not alone in that place, and that somebody had stolen their child. The mother let out a cry, exclaiming, "*Hánnuš* has taken our son!"

There was nothing they could do that night. They were freezing, and soon sleep came to them.

At dawn they gathered their things, and decided to go up the mountain in search of their son. They painted their faces and started the search.

It was not long before they heard a song, and laughter. They saw *hánnuš*, happy, dancing around the child, picking him up and taking a white powder in his hands and rubbing it over the boy's body. The frightened parents didn't dare to get close, but the moment that *hánnuš* put the boy down, so he could go to cut meat from a guanaco – perhaps to feed the boy, who he now considered to be his child – the father ran over and picked the boy up. Taking his wife by the arm, they all ran down to where their canoe was and headed out to sea.

When *hánnuš* turned around and saw that the boy wasn't there, he asked himself – *kúi kátakar kaióla*, "Where is the child?" In despair, he ran down to the place where he had taken the boy from.

Arriving at the shore, he saw that the canoe was already far away from him and that his child was in it. Nothing could stop the tears from pouring from his eyes, and he ran back and forth desperately, from one place to another. *Hánnuš* was alone again.

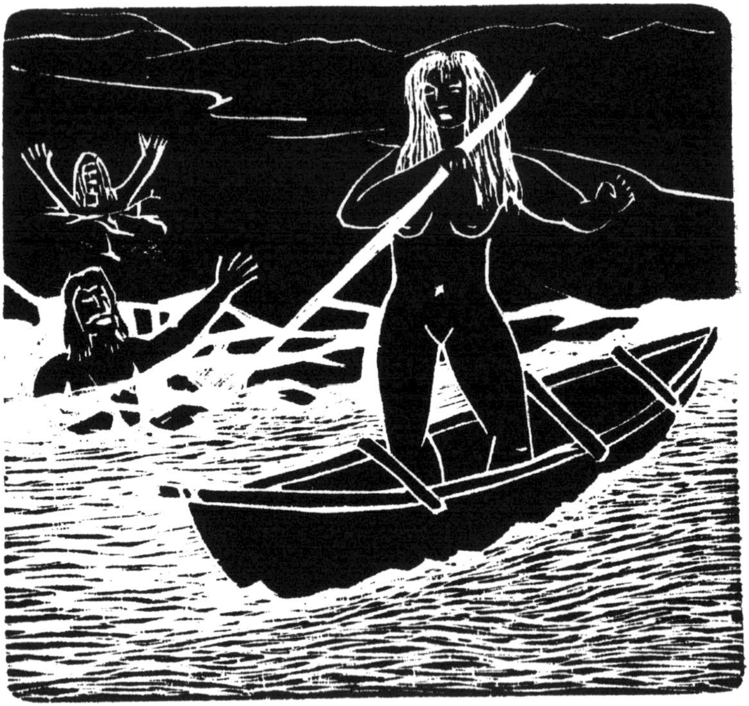

HÁNNUŠ AND THE WOMAN

Hánnuš was a constant presence for generations of Yagan. Even if he hadn't been seen for a long time, the Yagan never stopped feeling his *kašpíx*, the spirit of *hánnuš* who lived in the mountains. And when a *yámana* went walking up there, if he heard a horrible cry – "oohhh!" – he would have to keep going without looking back, keep going until he arrived at the seashore.

There is a story of a woman who was very cunning. She lived alone in a cabin that she had built herself. She made her cabin very strong, because *hánnuš* was always nearby, trying to make her fall in love with him. He wanted her to be his wife.

She did not want to be his wife. So, besides making her cabin very strong, she also constructed it with a low entranceway, and she lived underneath the floor. Because *hánnuš*, once he realized that she was always going to refuse him, threatened her – that he would round up all the other *hánnuš*, and go after her and kill her.

One day *hánnuš* came, her would-be lover, but now with this intention. He went into the cabin and spun round and round, searching for her. He could not find her, and he turned to go back out. But the woman was underneath him, armed with an urchin-spear. She aimed it at his genitals, and plucked them right out.

And this happened with many *hánnuš*. After this one, more *hánnuš* came, coming after this woman, and the same thing happened to each one. Even seeing one another so injured, more came anyway.

Until finally the woman decided to leave her home. One cold winter day, when the sea near the shore was covered by a layer of ice, she gathered her things. And so she left, carrying that same urchin-spear, and she went walking over the ice, breaking it up behind her.

When the *hánnuš* saw the woman was leaving, they ran down to catch up with her. One by one they walked over the thin ice, and fell through into the water. The woman threw herself into her canoe, managing to leave that place and at the same time killing all those *hánnuš*.

They tell a story of a man who surprised *hánnuš*. He chased *hánnuš* to a cliff, where *hánnuš* hid, suffering as the man threw stones at him, until the man finally killed *hánnuš*.

Today we talk about *Hánnuš Árkuř*, or "Monkey Cliff," located at Molinares on Hoste Island, where we can see the rock that reminds us of the presence of *hánnuš* living among the Yagan. A big tree grew on that rock.

kašpíx | Spirit

IV

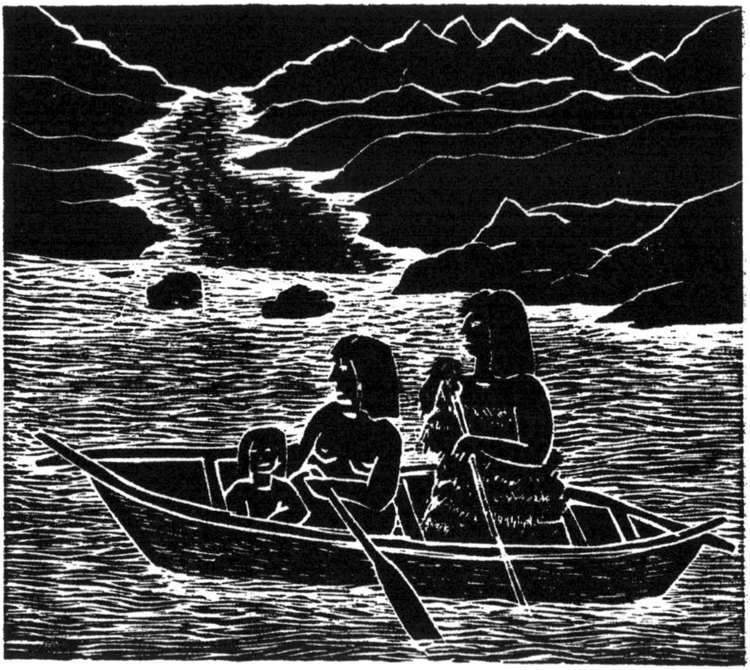

TÁUN OR GLACIERS

Back when we used to go paddling through the channels, I often went out with a grandmother who always had something to tell me. They used to say that if you went close to the icebergs you had to paint your face, and that you should not stare at the glaciers, because it is bad. I believe it, because I have seen it...

You are not supposed to play with the ice. It is people. The spirit of the man who died is there, he who was all-knowing and half-witch. All these spirits are there. If you go looking at it, it may suddenly break apart and water pours out.

One time my dad went to hunt a guanaco, in Puerto Olla. He cut a quarter of the guanaco to carry home. He had to cross an ice sheet, smooth like the floor, but wide, to get to the tent where my mom was. He told me that he was crossing, and just when he was half-way, the ice began to open itself up. He dropped the meat and went jumping across the pieces of ice, until he made it back to the tent. If he had fallen in there, he would have died.

Nobody believes me, I tell this story but nobody wants to believe me. I'm telling you what they told to me.

When I was a little girl, one time I went playing over there, alone on the beach. That was in Puerto Olla. I stopped, to look at a giant glacier. It was big like a house, just stuck there on the beach. It seemed that there were people inside it speaking, it sounded like they were cutting firewood with an axe. I was looking towards that glacier, but I couldn't see any people, just the big *táun*.

It didn't scare me. I went back to where my people were, to tell them what had happened. My brother and Esmelinda were there, and I told them where I had gone, and that I could hear voices in that glacier that was stuck there – that there were people talking inside it.

My brother said, "Yes, that happens." The others didn't want to believe me, but my brother had already warned me about this, that you must not play with the ice, that day that we found ourselves camped beside the big *táun*.

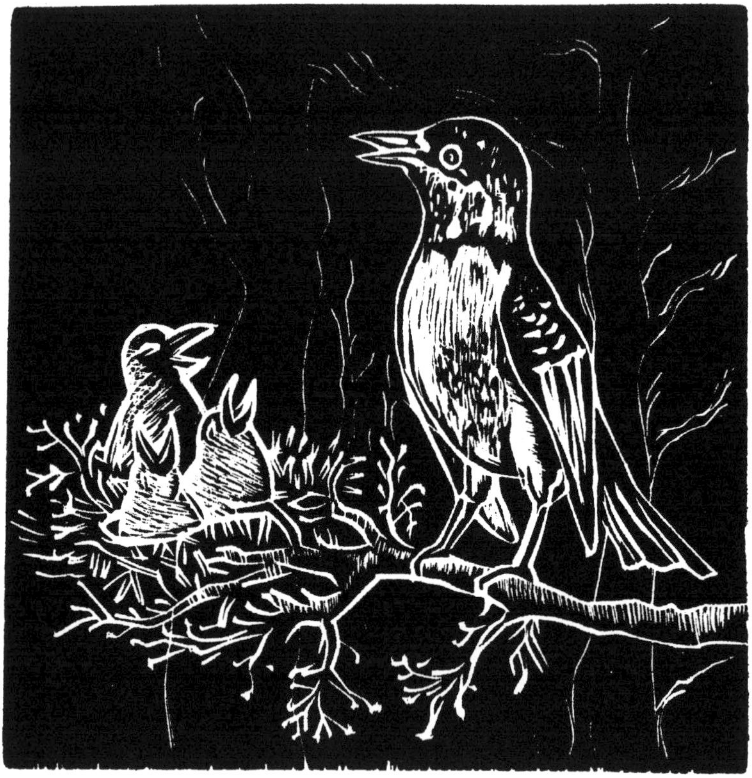

AKASIŘ OR THRUSH

They used to tell me that when the thrush has chicks, the mother teaches the oldest one – and that for other birds this happens as well – so that if the mother is no longer around, *akasiř* can take care of his younger brothers and sisters.

I went to see for myself. Stretched out on the ground, I watched the mother thrush. She flew up to a twig and was teaching her son, saying, "When you have a little brother, you must teach him, show him how to work, teach him to bathe himself." This is what the little bird was singing, and then they flew down to the river together where they bathed, washed themselves and shook themselves off, then returned to the same twig. And so they go, growing up.

If the young thrush doesn't listen to his mother and obey her, the mother abandons him. Left alone, the baby thrush doesn't have anything to eat, so he feeds on tree mushrooms, the digüeñes, but bad ones that are old, and they make him sick and he dies. That's why, in mid-winter, you can see in the mountains and on the shorelines these dead thrushes, the ones who disobeyed.

On the other hand, those who obey their mother grow up healthy, eating good fruits, like the berries of chaura and mema.

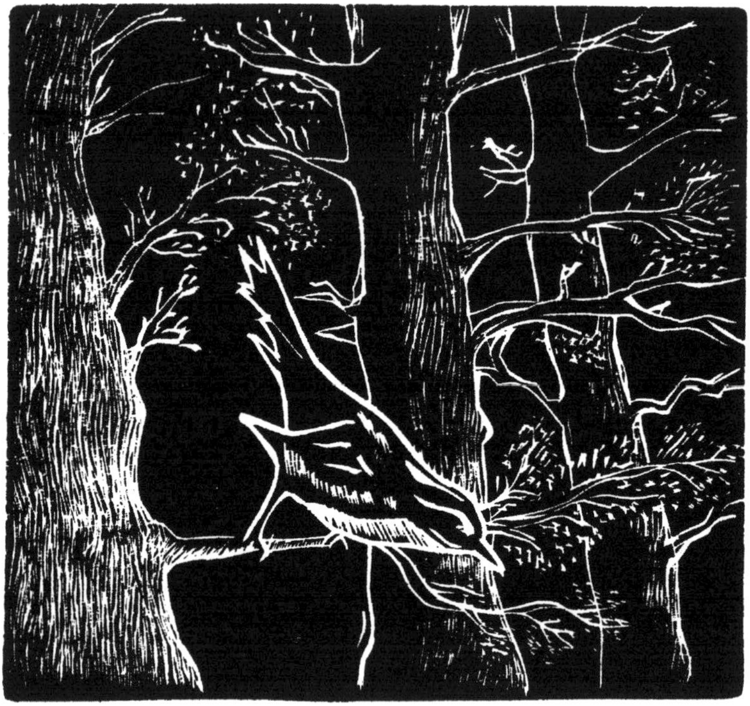

TAČIKÁČINA OR RAYADITO

Tačikáčina or rayadito is a little bird who sings on the mountain by day, letting us know that someone is hidden – maybe a bad man or a witch, somebody concealed. He lets the walker know that somebody is there.

Their cries, when they sing together, bring fear: "tsch-tsch-tsch-tsch," warning us of nothing good.

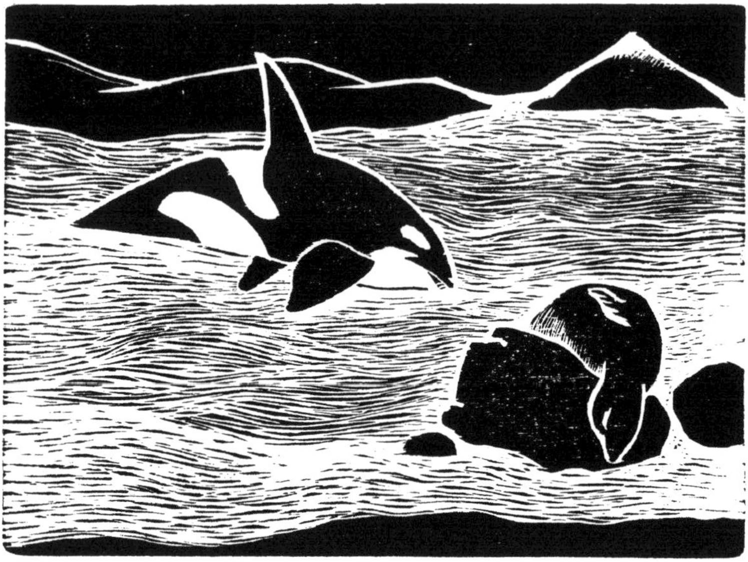

HAINÓLA OR ORCA

Our ancestors used to respect *hainóla* very much. He is like a person.

Once, a woman went to the edge of the beach. She turned towards *hainóla*, and said to him, "I feel like eating sea-lion, bring me one."

Hainóla responded to Mery's words by waving his fin.

Returning to her camp, she told everyone what had happened, but nobody believed her. The next day she returned to the beach with them. And from afar they could see that *hainóla* was pointing towards a rock with his fin, and on that rock they found the food, the sea-lion, as if it were waiting for her.

Hainóla was feared and respected by the Yagan, especially by married couples. Couples who were planning a canoe voyage through the channels had to avoid sexual relations the night before their voyage. If they did not watch themselves the night before, *hainóla* would surprise them and chase their canoes, making the voyage dangerous.

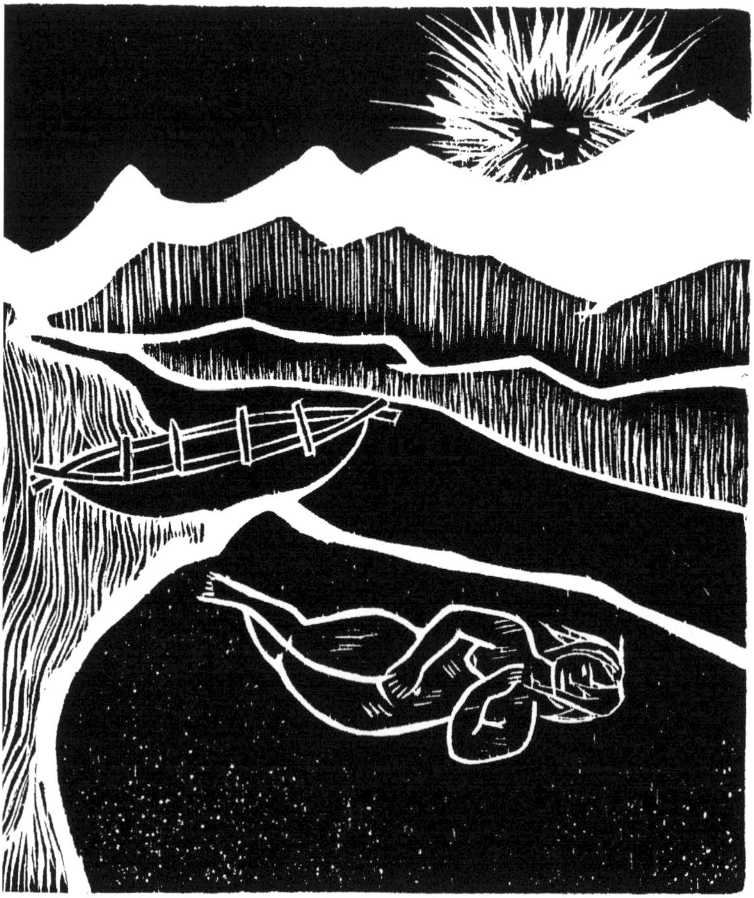

LUŠ YÁMANA OR SHINING MAN

There was a place where the Indians used to go in search of stone arrowheads. They had to always go as two men and one woman. The men would go to shore, and the woman would tie the canoe up in the kelp, and wait for them there.

While she was waiting for them, a beautiful man used to come down to her. He was *Lăm*, the sun. He would try to convince the young woman to get out of the canoe and come to him, but she never allowed herself to be overcome by the beauty of *Lăm*.

Soon, the men would come back, and the three of them would undertake their journey back home together.

Arriving back at camp, the men always talked about the good behaviour of this girl who accompanied them on their trips. They knew about this beautiful man.

And every time they went to that place, the same thing happened to this girl.

So one day, after hearing the words they said

about this girl, another young girl came along, telling them that she was as good or even better than the girl that they were talking about. The men could see that she was envious of that girl.

So they smiled and said, "Fine, tomorrow then, it will be you who comes with us."

The next day, they undertook the voyage. The men got out of the canoe, heading towards the mountain. The girl stayed in the canoe, and soon she saw a beautiful man who called to her. The girl slid out of the canoe immediately and went to him, and allowed passion to overcome her. Then the sun left. She stretched out on the seashore, content – then, violently, she scratched up her whole body.

Printed in Great Britain
by Amazon